Dhamma Verses

S.N. GOENKA

DHAMMA VERSES

poems of a modern-day
master of Vipassana meditation

Vippasana Research Publications • Seattle

Vipassana Research Publications
P.O. Box 15926
Seattle, WA 98115, U.S.A.
www.vrpa.com

Text transcribed and translated from Hindi *dohas* of S.N. Goenka, recorded at Bombay, India, February 29, 1986.

First edition, 2000

Printed in the United States of America

ISBN 0-9649484-4-3 (book & audio tape)

ISBN 0-9649484-7-8 (book)

Library of Congress Card Number: 99-69197 (book)

Publisher's Cataloging-in-Publication Data:
(provided by Quality Books, Inc.)

Goenka, S.N., 1924-
Dhamma verses : poems of a modern-day master of Vipassana meditation / S.N. Goenka. -- 1st ed.
p. cm.
"Hindi originals in Devanagari and Roman scripts with English translation."
LCCN: 99-69197
ISBN: 0-9649484-7-8

1. Vipasyana (Buddhism)--Poetry. 2. Buddhist poetry. 3. Couplets, Hindi. I. Title.

PK2098.22.O45D43 2000 891.4'3172
QBI99-1892

सुनो कान-वालों सुनो,
सत्य धर्म का सार।

Suno kāna-valoṅ suno,
satya Dharma kā sāra!

Let those with ears hearken
to the essence of true Dhamma!

S.N. Goenka

Preface

THE AUTHOR OF THESE VERSES is best known as a modern representative of an ancient spiritual tradition dating back millennia. But S.N. Goenka carries on another tradition as well: that of the poet-sage whose words point the way to higher things. In India, from the time of the Buddha to the present, poetry on spiritual themes has flourished through the generations, and many leading spiritual figures are remembered equally for their literary compositions.

For the genre a particular form has evolved: that of the *doha* or couplet. As the name indicates, this is a two-line verse, with a pause in the middle of each line. The result is a stanza that, to Western ears, sounds remarkably similar to the ballad form. Like the ballad in Europe and America, the *doha* has been the vehicle for folk poetry in India. In both cases the form seems peculiarly suited to its language and culture, allowing it to become the medium for popular expression.

This is the rich tradition from which spring the *dohas* of S.N. Goenka. Elsewhere he has recounted how his grandfather composed *dohas*, and how he himself tried his hand when still a schoolboy. Later, when he began to teach Vipassana meditation, he put his gift to good use. Since 1969, tens of thousands of people participating in Vipassana courses have gained inspiration and understanding from the *dohas* recited by him.

His compositions all deal with one subject: what in Hindi or Sanskrit is called *dharma,* a word that has been borrowed into English. In modern Indian usage this commonly means religion; one can talk of Hindu *dharma,* Jain *dharma,* Sikh *dharma* and so on. In English the word is much more vague but is often used to denote any religious practice derived from Indian tradition.

For S.N. Goenka, neither usage is satisfactory. He employs the Hindi word *dharma* in a different, highly specific way. At the most basic level, the word means nature or natural phenomenon. From this the meaning has extended to refer to the rules that govern such phenomena—that is, the laws of nature. In Indian tradition, these laws are seen as applying not only in the physical but also in the mental, moral and spiritual spheres. Hence the word has come to mean spiritual laws, especially the teaching by which to achieve liberation.

This is how the Buddha used the term; and so, to translate it, we have chosen *dhamma*—the word as it appears in Pāli, the language actually spoken by the Buddha twenty-five centuries ago.

What, then, is the Dhamma, the teaching of liberation? A vast literature records it, but to paraphrase the

Buddha, the Dhamma can be summed up very simply: this is suffering, and this is the way out of suffering.

According to the Dhamma, suffering is an unavoidable part of existence; and it has its origin in how the mind works. Suffering results from our own actions (Pāli *kamma*). It arises because, out of ignorance, we indulge in craving or its reverse of aversion—specifically, the craving for pleasant experiences and aversion toward unpleasant ones. The conditioning of the mind is to react with craving or aversion toward whatever it encounters; and every reaction leads to tension and strengthens this unhealthy habit pattern. If the pattern can be broken, there will be no reaction and no resulting tension or suffering. One lives a happy, balanced life and step by step approaches the experience of the unconditioned, *nibbāna* —a state that is beyond all suffering.

Vipassana ("insight") meditation is the way to bring about this mental transformation. It involves three stages or trainings. The first is *sīla,* or moral conduct. This is the foundation of the practice; it involves avoiding any physical or vocal action that can harm others. The second training is *samādhi,* concentration or mastery of the mind. It is the effort to keep the mind on a chosen object of attention. In a Vipassana course this object is the natural breath entering and leaving the nostrils—and when the mind wanders off, the instruction is to bring it back as quickly as possible. In this way the meditator learns to avoid distractions and take control of the mind, keeping it fixed on the reality of the present moment.

The third training is *paññā,* or wisdom. Having learned to concentrate the mind, the meditator now systematically shifts the attention throughout the physical structure, focusing on each area in turn. In each the effort is to remain aware of the physical sensations naturally occurring—to remain aware and not react to them, understanding their impermanent nature.

This focus on sensation is the special feature of the teaching of the Buddha. Many other spiritual figures have taught the necessity of moral conduct and mental mastery. Many have explained the need to avoid reactions of craving and aversion in order to avoid suffering. The Buddha showed a practical way to do this. He realized that we react not to outside phenomena but to the sensations that they provoke within ourselves. By learning to observe all sensations dispassionately, we stop the process of reaction—that is, of conditioning—and we allow deconditioning to begin. Gradually we weaken the mental habit pattern of reacting. We learn not to be overwhelmed by what we experience, whether physical or mental, and thus we develop real detachment.

As conditioning ceases, suffering ceases. We begin to enjoy the happiness of liberation. The mind fills with good will for others, joy in their success, compassion for their failings and equanimity toward all that comes one's way in life. We find an inner peace, and every action we take naturally fosters peace all around.

Such in brief is the Dhamma—as S.N. Goenka has often called it, an art of living. Learning this art is the purpose of Vipassana meditation. To those who practice it, the *dohas* offer encouragement, inspiration and elucidation of the path. To others they provide an understanding of the teaching of liberation.

The tape here transcribed records S.N. Goenka reciting some of his most memorable Hindi *dohas*. With one or two exceptions he chants each twice, often with the wording varied in the repetition. Since it is usually minor in nature, the variant has been ignored in the transcription and translation. Where it is of more significance, both versions are given.

The Hindi text is presented in the traditional Devanāgarī and (for those who cannot read it) in Roman script. Since the verse line is quite long and the pause naturally divides it into two, the *doha* sounds to Western ears like four short lines rather than two long ones; and that is the format used here.

The English attempts to follow the Hindi closely while giving a sense of the beauty and power of the original. At the end are a few notes of explanation as needed.

This work has been germinating for more than a decade, and many have had a hand in helping it develop. They include the late B.P. Paliwal, Thomas Crisman, S.N. Tandon and others. My gratitude to all of them, and especially to S.N. Goenka for composing these verses and transmitting the matchless teaching they express.

—William Hart, Ottawa 1999

Pronunciation of Romanized Hindi

Hindi is written in Devanāgarī, a descendant of the Brahmī script that was well established in India before 500 BC. Written from left to right, the script is generally phonetic in nature. In Roman script diacritical marks are added to indicate the proper pronunciation of Hindi, as follows.

The alphabet consists of forty-six basic characters: twelve vowels plus the *anusvāra,* which is a nasalization of each vowel sound, and thirty-three consonants.

Vowels: a, ā, i, ī, u, ū, e, o, ai, au, ḥ, ṛ

Consonants:

Velar:	k	kh	g	gh	ṅ
Palatal:	c	ch	j	jh	ñ
Retroflex:	ṭ	ṭh	ḍ	ḍh	ṇ
Dental:	t	th	d	dh	n
Labial:	p	ph	b	bh	m
Miscellaneous:		y, r, l, v, ś, ṣ, s, h			

The vowels **a, i, u** are short; **ā, ī, ū** are long. Pronunciation is as follows:

a like "a" in "about" **ā** like "a" in "father"
i like "i" in "mint" **ī** like "ee" in "see"
u like "u" in "put" **ū** like "oo" in "pool"

The vowel **e** is pronounced like the "e" in "they"; **o** like the "o" in "tone."

The vowels represented by the diphthongs **ai,** and **au** are pronounced as they would be in English: **ai** like "aee" and **au** like the "ou" in "loud." Note that **ie** and **ae** are not dipthongs; in each case the two vowels are pronounced separately.

ḥ—an aspiration following the vowel, e.g., "aḥ" is like "uh"

ṛ—a vocalized "r" pronounced like "ri" with a rolled "r"

The consonant **c** is soft as in the "ch" in "church." All the aspirated consonants are pronounced with an audible expulsion of breath following the normal unaspirated sound. Therefore **th** is not as in "three" but more like the sound in "Thailand," and **ph** is not as in "photo" but rather is pronounced "p" accompanied by an expulsion of breath.

The retroflex consonants **ṭ, ṭh, ḍ, ḍh, ṇ** are pronounced with the tip of the tongue turned back, whereas in the dentals **t, th, d, dh, n,** it touches the upper front teeth.

The palatal nasal, **ñ,** is the same as the Spanish "ñ" as in *señor*. The velar nasal, **ṅ,** is pronounced like "ng" in "singer." The *anusvāra* nasalizations are presented in various forms (**n, ṅ, ñ, ṇ, m** or **ṃ**), as seems appropriate to approximate the proper sound for an English speaker.

The Hindi **v** is a soft "v" or "w."

Ś is pronounced "sh" and **ṣ** is a retroflex "sh" pronounced with the tongue turned back.

Dohas

Hindi originals transcribed
in Devanāgarī and Roman scripts
with English translation

SIDE A

१

जागो लोगो जगत के,
बीती काली रात।
हुआ उजाला धरम का,
मंगल हुआ प्रभात।।

Jāgo logo jagata ke,
bītī kālī rāta.
Huā ujālā Dharama kā,
maṅgala huā prabhāta.

२

आओ प्राणी विश्व के,
सुनो धरम का ज्ञान।
इसमें सुख है शांति है,
मुक्ति मोक्ष निरवाण।।

Āo prāṇī viśva ke,
suno Dharama kā gyāna.
Isameṅ sukha hai śānti hai,
mukti, mokṣa, niravāṇa.

३

यह तो वाणी धरम की,
बोधि ज्ञान की ज्योत।
अक्षर अक्षर में भरा,
मंगल ओतपरोत।।

Yaha to vāṇī Dharama kī,
bodhi gyāna kī jyota.
Akṣara akṣara meṅ bharā,
maṅgala otaparota.

४

मीठी वाणी धरम की,
मिसरी के से बोल।
कल्याणी मंगलमयी,
भरा अमृतरस घोल।।

Mīṭhī vāṇī Dharama kī,
misarī ke se bola.
Kalyāṇī maṅgalamayī,
bharā amṛtarasa ghola.

SIDE A

1
People of the world, awake!
The dark night is over.
The light has come of Dhamma,
the dawn of happiness.

2
Come, beings of the universe!
Listen to the wisdom of the Dhamma.
In this lies happiness and peace,
liberation, deliverance, *nibbāna.*

3
These are the words of Dhamma,
the flame of enlightenment-wisdom,
each syllable of them filled
and permeated with happiness.

4
Sweet are the words of Dhamma,
each phrase like crystallized sugar,
yielding welfare and happiness,
suffused with the taste of the deathless.

५

आओ मानव मानवी,	Āo mānava mānavī,
चलें धरम के पंथ।	caleṅ Dharama ke pantha.
इस पथ चलते सत्पुरुष,	Isa patha calate satpuruṣa,
इस पथ चलते संत।।	isa patha calate santa.

६

धरम पंथ ही शांति पथ,	Dharama pantha hī śānti patha,
धरम पंथ सुख पंथ।	Dharama pantha sukha pantha.
धरम पंथ पर जो चले,	Dharama pantha para jo cale,
करे दुखों का अंत।।	kare dukhoṅ kā anta.

७

इस पथ मंगल मूल है,	Isa patha maṅgala mūla hai,
इस पथ है कल्याण।	isa patha hai kalyāṇa.
इस पथ पर जो भी चले,	Isa patha para jo bhī cale,
पाय सुखों की खान।।	pāya sukhoṅ kī khāna.

८

धरम धरम तो सब कहें,	Dharama Dharama to saba kaheṅ,
पर समझे ना कोय।	para samajhe nā koya.
शुद्ध चित्त का आचरण,	Śuddha citta kā ācaraṇa,
शुद्ध धरम है सोय।।	śuddha Dharama hai soya.

5
Come, men and women!
Let us walk the path of Dhamma.
On this path walk holy ones,
on this path walk saints.

6
The path of Dhamma is the path of peace,
the path of Dhamma is the path of happiness.
Whoever walks the path of Dhamma
makes an end of suffering.

7
This path is the source of well-being,
this is the path of welfare.
Whoever walks upon this path
finds a storehouse of happiness.

8
Everyone talks about Dhamma
but no one understands it.
Practicing purity of mind—
this is true Dhamma.

९
मैं भी दुखिया ना रहूं,
जगत दुखी ना होय।
जीवन जीने की कला,
सत्य धरम है सोय।।

Maiṅ bhī dukhiyā nā rahūṅ,
jagata dukhī nā hoya.
Jīvana jīne kī kalā,
satya Dharama hai soya.

१०
धरम न हिंदू बौद्ध है,
सिक्ख न मुसलिम जैन।
धरम चित्त की शुद्धता,
धरम शांति सुख चैन।।

Dharama na Hindū Bauddha hai,
Sikkha na Musalima Jaina.
Dharama citta kī śuddhatā,
Dharama śānti sukha caina.

११
संप्रदाय ना धरम है,
धरम न बने दिवार।
धरम सिखाए एकता,
धरम सिखाए प्यार।।

Sampradāya nā Dharama hai,
Dharama na bane divāra.
Dharama sikhāe ekatā,
Dharama sikhāe pyāra.

१२
जात पांत ना धरम है,
धरम न छूआछूत।
धरम पंथ पर जो चले,
होवे पावन पूत।।

Jāta pānta nā Dharama hai,
Dharama na chūā-chūta.
Dharama pantha para jo cale,
hove pāvana pūta.

9

May I and may the world
be without suffering;
this is the art of living,
this is true Dhamma.

10

Dhamma is not Hindu or Buddhist,
not Sikh, Muslim or Jain;
Dhamma is purity of heart,
peace, happiness, serenity.

11

Sectarianism is not Dhamma;
Dhamma raises no walls.
Dhamma teaches oneness,
Dhamma teaches love.

12

Caste or rank is not Dhamma,
Dhamma is not untouchability.
Whoever walks the path of Dhamma
becomes a holy person.

१३

जाति वर्ण का गोत्र का, जहां भेद ना होय। जो सबका सबके लिए, धरम शुद्ध है सोय।।	Jāti varṇa kā gotra kā, jahāṅ bheda nā hoya. Jo sabakā sabake lie, Dharama śuddha hai soya.

१४

मानव मानव में जहां, भेदभाव ना होय। निजहित परहित सर्वहित, सत्य धरम है सोय।।	Mānava mānava meṅ jahāṅ, bhedabhāva nā hoya. Nijahita parahita sarvahita, satya Dharama hai soya.

१५

अपना भी होवे भला, भला सभी का होय। जिससे जग का हो भला, शुद्ध धरम है सोय।।	Apanā bhī hove bhalā, bhalā sabhī kā hoya. Jisase jaga kā ho bhalā, śuddha Dharama hai soya.

१६

धन्य होंय माता पिता, धन्य होंय कुल गोत। धर्मपुरुष जनमें जहां, लिये ज्ञान की ज्योत।।	Dhanya hoṅya mātā pitā, dhanya hoṅya kula gota. Dharma puruṣa janameṅ jahāṅ, liye gyāna kī jyota.

13
Between caste, class or clan
making no distinction;
for one and all—
this is pure Dhamma.

14
Between one person and another
making no distinction;
of benefit to oneself, to others, to all—
this is true Dhamma.

15
Good for oneself,
good for everyone,
good for the world—
this is pure Dhamma.

16
Fortunate the mother and father,
fortunate the family and clan
to whom is born a man of Dhamma
bearing the torch of wisdom.

१७

यही धरम की परख है,
यही धरम का माप।
जन जन का मंगल करे,
दूर करे संताप।।

Yahī Dharama kī parakha hai,
yahī Dharama kā māpa.
Jana jana kā maṅgala kare,
dūra kare santāpa.

१८

कुदरत का कानून है,
इससे बचा न कोय।
मैले मन व्याकुल रहे,
निरमल सुखिया होय।।

Kudarata kā kānūna hai,
isase bacā na koya.
Maile mana vyākula rahe,
niramala sukhiyā hoya.

१९

यह ऋत है, यह नियम है,
सब पर लागू होय।
धर्म धार सुख ही मिले,
छूटे दुख ही होय।।

Yaha ṛta hai, yaha niyama hai,
saba para lāgū hoya.
Dharma dhāra sukha hī mile,
chūṭe dukha hī hoya.

२०

निरधन या धनवान हो,
अनपढ़ या विदवान।
जिसने मन मैला किया,
उसके व्याकुल प्राण।।

Niradhana yā dhanavāna ho,
anapaḍha yā vidavāna.
Jisane mana mailā kiyā,
usake vyākula prāṇa.

17
This is the only test of Dhamma,
this is its only measure:
for everyone it provides well-being
and removes suffering.

18
This is the law of nature,
which no one can escape:
a defiled mind remains agitated,
an unstained mind is happy.

19
This is the law, the rule,
which applies to one and all:
if you practice Dhamma you find happiness,
if you forsake it you are miserable.

20
Poor or rich,
illiterate or learnèd,
whoever has defiled his mind
is troubled in spirit.

२१

हिंदू हो या बौद्ध हो,	Hindū ho yā Bauddha ho,
मुसलिम हो या जैन।	Musalima ho yā Jaina.
जब जब मन मैला करे,	Jaba jaba mana mailā kare,
तब तब हो बेचैन।।	taba taba ho becaina.

२२

गोरा काला गेहुंआ,	Gorā kālā gehuṅā,
मनुज मनुज ही होय।	manuja manuja hī hoya.
जो जो मन मैला करे,	Jo jo mana mailā kare,
सो ही दुखिया होय।।	so hī dukhiyā hoya.

२३

वर्ण रंग से मानवी,	Varṇa raṅga se mānavī,
ऊंच नीच ना होय।	ūñca nīca nā hoya.
काली गोरी गाय का,	Kālī gorī gāya kā,
दूध एक सा होय।।	dūdha eka sā hoya.

२४

धर्मवंत तो है वही,	Dharmavanta to hai vahī,
शीलवंत जो होय।	śīlavanta jo hoya.
काया वाणी चित्त के,	Kāyā vāṇī citta ke,
शील न खंडित होंय।।	śīla na khaṇḍita hoṅya.

21
Hindu or Buddhist,
Muslim or Jain,
whenever you defile your mind
you become agitated.

22
White, black or brown,
a man is still a man.
Whoever defiles his mind
becomes miserable.

23
The color of a man's skin
makes him neither high nor low.
Black or white, a cow
gives milk all the same.

24
To practice the Dhamma
one must practice *sīla*.
Not by body, speech or mind
should *sīla* be broken.

२५

कायिक कर्म सुधार ले,
वाचिक कर्म सुधार।
मनसा कर्म सुधार ले,
यही धरम का सार।।

Kāyika karma sudhāra le,
vācika karma sudhāra.
Manasā karma sudhāra le,
yahī Dharama kā sāra.

२६(क)

सदाचरण ही धरम है,
दुराचरण ही पाप।
सदाचरण से सुख जगे,
दुराचरण दुख ताप।।

Sadācaraṇa hī Dharama hai,
durācaraṇa hī pāpa.
Sadācaraṇa se sukha jage,
durācaraṇa dukha tāpa.

२६(ख)

परोपकार ही पुण्य है,
पर-पीड़न ही पाप।
पुण्य किये सुख ही जगे,
पाप किये संताप।।

Paropakāra hī puṇya hai,
para-pīḍana hī pāpa.
Puṇya kiye sukha hī jage,
pāpa kiye santāpa.

२७

तीन बात बंधन बंधें,
राग द्वेष अभिमान।
तीन बात बंधन खुलें,
शील समाधि ज्ञान।।

Tīna bāta bandhana bandheṅ,
rāga dveṣa abhimāna.
Tīna bāta bandhana khuleṅ,
śīla samādhi gyāna.

25

Transform your deeds of body,
transform your deeds of speech,
transform your mental deeds—
this is the essence of Dhamma.

26a

Right action is Dhamma,
wrong action is sin.
From right action comes happiness;
from wrong action, suffering and torment.

26b

Helping others is virtue;
harming others is sin.
Virtue brings happiness;
sin causes torment.

27

Threefold is our bondage:
craving, aversion, egotism.
Threefold is the deliverance:
morality, concentration and wisdom.

२८

प्रज्ञा शील समाधि की,	Pragyā śīla samādhi kī,
बहे त्रिवेणी धार।	bahe triveṇī dhāra.
डुबकी मारे सो तिरे,	Ḍubakī māre so tire,
हो भव सागर पार।।	ho bhava sāgara pāra.

२९

गंगा जमुना सरस्वती,	Gaṅgā Jamunā Sarasvatī,
शील समाधि ज्ञान।	śīla samādhi gyāna.
तीनों का संगम होवे,	Tīnoṅ kā saṅgama hove,
प्रगटे पद निरवाण।।	pragaṭe pada niravāṇa.

३०

शील-धरम पालन भला,	Śīla-dharama pālana bhalā,
निरमल भली समाधि।	niramala bhalī samādhi.
प्रज्ञा तो जाग्रत भली,	Pragyā to jāgrata bhalī,
दूर करे भव व्याधि।।	dūra kare bhava vyādhi.

३१

शील हमारे पुष्ट हों,	Śīla hamāre puṣṭa hoṅ,
होवे चित्त अडोल।	hove citta aḍola.
प्रज्ञा जागे बींधती,	Pragyā jāge bīndhatī,
देय ग्रंथियां खोल।।	deya granthiyāṅ khola.

28
Morality, concentration, and wisdom—
three streams have joined together.
By plunging into their confluence
you cross the ocean of suffering.

29
The true Ganges, Jamuna and Saraswati
are morality, concentration and wisdom.
Where the three converge
nibbāna manifests.

30
Good to practice morality,
good is right concentration,
good is the awakening of insight
to cure the ills of life.

31
May we be strong in moral conduct,
may our minds be unwavering,
may penetrating insight arise
to untie our bonds.

३२

धर्म छुटे तो सुख छुटे,
आकुल व्याकुल होय।
धर्म जगे तो सुख जगे,
हरखित पुलकित होय।।

Dharma chuṭe to sukha chuṭe,
ākula vyākula hoya.
Dharma jage to sukha jage,
harakhita pulakita hoya.

३३

मंगल मंगल धरम का,
मंगल ही फल होय।
अंतर की गांठें खुलें,
मानस निरमल होय।।

Maṅgala maṅgala Dharama kā,
maṅgala hī phala hoya.
Antara kī gāṇṭheṅ khuleṅ,
mānasa niramala hoya.

३४

अंतर गंगा धरम की,
लहर लहर लहराय।
राग द्वेष के मोह के,
मैल सभी धुल जांय।।

Antara Gaṅgā Dharama kī,
lahara lahara laharāya.
Rāga dveṣa ke moha ke,
maila sabhī dhula jāṅya.

३५

जीएं जीवन धरम का,
रहें पाप से दूर।
चित धारा निरमल रहे,
मंगल से भरपूर।।

Jieṅ jīvana Dharama kā,
raheṅ pāpa se dūra.
Cita dhārā niramala rahe,
maṅgala se bharapūra.

32
If Dhamma is lost, happiness is lost:
you are anxious and agitated.
If Dhamma arises, happiness arises:
you are filled with joy and bliss.

33
The all-auspicious Dhamma
bears auspicious fruit.
Knots within are opened,
the mind becomes stainless.

34
May the Ganges of Dhamma within
keep flowing, flowing, flowing,
to wash away all the stains
of craving, aversion and ignorance.

35
Live the life of Dhamma,
keep far away from evil,
keep unsullied the flow of mind,
and brim over with happiness.

३६

धरमविहारी पुरुष हों,
धरमचारिणी नार।
धरमवंत संतान हो,
सुखी रहे परिवार।।

Dharama vihārī puruṣa hoṅ,
Dharamacāriṇī nāra.
Dharamavanta santāna ho,
sukhī rahe parivāra.

३७

धरम सदा मंगल करे,
धरम करे कल्याण।
धर्म सदा रक्षा करे,
धरम बड़ा बलवान।।

Dharama sadā maṅgala kare,
Dharama kare kalyāṇa.
Dharma sadā rakṣā kare,
Dharama baḍā balavāna.

३८

धरम सदृश रक्षक नहीं,
धरम सदृश नहीं ढाल।
धरम पालकों की सदा,
धरम करे प्रतिपाल।।

Dharama sadṛśa rakṣaka nahīṅ,
Dharama sadṛśa nahīṅ ḍhāla.
Dharama pālakoṅ kī sadā,
Dharama kare pratipāla.

३९

प्रलयंकारी बाढ़ में,
धरम सदृश ना द्वीप।
काल अंधेरी रात में,
धरम सदृश ना दीप।।

Pralayaṅkārī bāḍha meṅ,
Dharama sadṛśa nā dvīpa.
Kāla andherī rāta meṅ,
Dharama sadṛśa nā dīpa.

36
May the husband dwell in Dhamma,
may the wife walk in Dhamma,
may the children be full of Dhamma
to keep the family happy.

37
Dhamma always gives happiness,
Dhamma always gives welfare.
Dhamma always gives protection;
great is the power of Dhamma.

38
There is no protector like Dhamma,
there is no shield like Dhamma.
The Dhamma always keeps secure
those who keep the Dhamma.

39
In the all-destroying deluge
there is no island like the Dhamma.
In the pitch-black night
there is no lamp like the Dhamma.

४०
धरम हमारा ईशवर,
धरम हमारा नाथ।
सदा सुरक्षित ही रहें,
धरम हमारे साथ।।

Dharama hamārā īśavara,
Dharama hamārā nātha.
Sadā surakṣita hī raheṅ,
Dharama hamāre sātha.

४१
धरम हमारा बंधु है,
सखा सहायक मीत।
चलें धरम की रीत ही,
रहे धरम से प्रीत।।

Dharama hamārā bandhu hai,
sakhā sahāyaka mīta.
Caleṅ Dharama kī rīta hī,
rahe Dharama se prīta.

४२
धर्म धार निरमल बने,
राजा हो या रंक।
रोग शोक चिंता मिटे,
निरभय बने निशंक।।

Dharma dhāra niramala bane,
rājā ho yā raṅka.
Roga śoka cintā miṭe,
nirabhaya bane niśaṅka.

४३
यही धरम का नियम है,
यही धरम की रीत।
जो धारे निरमल बने,
पावन बने पुनीत।।

Yahī Dharama kā niyama hai,
yahī Dharama kī rīta.
Jo dhāre niramala bane,
pāvana bane punīta.

40
Dhamma is our master,
Dhamma is our lord.
We are always protected
if Dhamma is with us.

41
Dhamma is our kin,
companion, helpmate, friend.
Let us walk to the measure of Dhamma,
giving our love to Dhamma.

42
Practice the Dhamma and become pure,
whether prince or pauper.
Sickness, sorrow and worry vanish;
no more fear or preplexity.

43
This is the law of Dhamma,
this is the way of Dhamma:
whoever applies it becomes pure,
holy and saintly.

४४

धर्म न मंदिर में मिले,	Dharma na mandira meṅ mile,
धर्म न हाट बिकाय।	Dharma na hāṭa bikāya.
धर्म न ग्रंथों में मिले,	Dharma na granthoṅ meṅ mile,
जो धारे सो पाय।।	jo dhāre so pāya.

४५

अपना रक्षित धरम ही,	Apanā rakṣita Dharama hī,
अपना रक्षक होय।	apanā rakṣaka hoya.
धारण कर लें धरम को,	Dhāraṇa kara leṅ Dharama ko,
धरम सहायक होय।।	Dharama sahāyaka hoya.

४६

वाणी तो वश में भली,	Vāṇī to vaśa meṅ bhalī,
वश में भला शरीर।	vaśa meṅ bhalā śarīra.
पर जो मन वश में करे,	Para jo mana vaśa meṅ kare,
वही शूर वह वीर।।	vahī śūra vaha vīra.

४७

मन ही दुरजन, मन सुजन,	Mana hī durajana, mana sujana,
मन बैरी, मन मीत।	mana bairī, mana mīta.
मन सुधरे सब सुधरि हैं,	Mana sudhare saba sudhari haiṅ,
कर मन परम पुनीत।।	kara mana parama punīta.

44
Dhamma is not found in temples,
or sold in the bazaar.
Dhamma is not found in books;
whoever applies it attains it.

45
Only if you guard the Dhamma
it will be your guard.
If you practice Dhamma,
the Dhamma is your helper.

46
Good to have mastery of speech,
good to have physical mastery,
but he who is master of his mind
is a warrior of real courage.

47
The mind can be wicked, the mind can be gentle,
the mind can be a foe or friend.
If the mind is transformed all is transformed,
so make your mind truly pure.

४८

मन बंधन का मूल है,
मन ही मुक्ति उपाय।
विकृत मन जकड़ा रहे,
निरविकार खुल जाय।।

Mana bandhana kā mūla hai,
mana hī mukti upāya.
Vikṛta mana jakaḍā rahe,
niravikāra khula jāya.

४९

मन चंचल मन चपल है,
भाग रहा सब ओर।
सांस डोर से बांध कर,
रोक राख इक ठोर।।

Mana cañcala mana capala hai,
bhāga rahā saba ora.
Sāṅsa ḍora se bāndha kara,
roka rākha ika ṭhora.

५०

जितना बुरा न कर सके,
दुशमन द्वेषी दोय।
अधिक बुरा निज मन करे,
जब यह मैला होय।।

Jitanā burā na kara sake,
duśamana dveṣī doya.
Adhika burā nija mana kare,
jaba yaha mailā hoya.

५१

जितना भला न कर सके,
मां बापु सब कोय।
अधिक भला निज मन करे,
जब मन उजला होय।।

Jitanā bhalā na kara sake,
māṅ bāpu saba koya.
Adhika bhalā nija mana kare,
jaba mana ujalā hoya.

48
Mind is the root of our bondage,
mind is the means of our liberation.
A polluted mind remains shackled,
an unpolluted mind becomes freed.

49
The mind is volatile and flighty,
wandering in every direction.
Bind it with a chain of breaths;
confine it to one point.

50
Neither enemy nor antagonist
can harm you as much
as can your own mind
when it is defiled.

51
Neither mother, father nor anyone
can do you as much good
as can your own mind
when it is bright and clear.

५२

मन के करम सुधार ले,	Mana ke karama sudhāra le,
मन ही प्रमुख प्रधान।	mana hī pramukha pradhāna.
कायिक वाचिक करम तो,	Kāyika vācika karama to,
मन की ही संतान।।	mana kī hī santāna.

५३

जो चाहे बंधन खुलें,	Jo cāhe bandhana khuleṅ,
मुक्ति दुखों से होय।	mukti dukhoṅ se hoya.
वश में कर ले चित्त को,	Vaśa meṅ kara le citta ko,
चित के वश मत होय।।	cita ke vaśa mata hoya.

५४

चित से चित का दमन कर,	Cita se cita kā damana kara,
चित से चित्त सुधार।	cita se citta sudhāra.
चित्त स्वच्छ कर चित्त से,	Citta svaccha kara citta se,
खोल मुक्ति के द्वार।।	khola mukti ke dvāra.

५५

चित की जैसी चेतना,	Cita kī jaisī cetanā,
फल वैसा ही होय।	phala vaisā hī hoya.
दुर्मन का फल दुखद ही,	Durmana kā phala dukhada hī,
सुखद सुमन का होय।।	sukhada sumana kā hoya.

52
Correct your mental actions;
mind is first and foremost.
Deeds of body and speech
are offspring of the mind.

53
If you seek release from bondage
and freedom from suffering,
be master of your mind;
do not be mastered by it.

54
By mind control your mind,
by mind transform your mind,
by mind cleanse your mind,
and open the door to liberation.

55
As is the volition of your mind,
so will be the fruit;
an impure mind yields fruits of misery,
a pure mind gives happiness.

५६

अपने अपने करम के,
हम ही तो करतार।
अपने सुख के दुःख के,
हम ही जिम्मेदार।।

Apane apane karama ke,
hama hī to karatāra.
Apane sukha ke duḥkha ke,
hama hī jimmedāra.

५७

जब तक मन में राग है,
जब तक मन में द्वेष।
तब तक दुख ही दुःख है,
मिटें न मन के क्लेश।।

Jaba taka mana meṅ rāga hai,
jaba taka mana meṅ dveṣa.
Taba taka dukha hī duḥkha hai,
miṭeṅ na mana ke kleśa.

५८

जितना गहरा राग है,
उतना गहरा द्वेष।
जितना गहरा द्वेष है,
उतना गहरा क्लेश।।

Jitanā gaharā rāga hai,
utanā gaharā dveṣa.
Jitanā gaharā dveṣa hai,
utanā gaharā kleśa.

५९

राग सदृश ना रोग है,
द्वेष सदृश ना दोष।
मोह सदृश ना मूढ़ता,
धरम सदृश ना होश।।

Rāga sadṛśa nā roga hai,
dveṣa sadṛśa nā doṣa.
Moha sadṛśa nā mūḍhatā,
Dharama sadṛśa nā hośa.

56
Of our own actions
we ourselves are the authors.
For our happiness or unhappiness
we alone are responsible.

57
As long as there is craving in the mind,
as long as in the mind is aversion,
there will be suffering, only suffering;
the mind cannot be purged of affliction.

58
Deeper the craving,
deeper is the aversion.
Deeper the aversion,
deeper is the affliction.

59
There is no disease like craving,
there is no frailty like aversion,
there is no folly like ignorance,
there is no sanity like Dhamma.

६०

क्षण क्षण जागे धरम ही,
क्षण क्षण जागे होश।
क्षण भर भी अज्ञान में,
रहें नहीं मदहोश।।

Kṣaṇa kṣaṇa jāge Dharama hī,
kṣaṇa kṣaṇa jāge hośa.
Kṣaṇa bhara bhī agyāna meṅ,
raheṅ nahīṅ madahośa.

६१

क्षण क्षण क्षण क्षण बीतते,
जीवन बीता जाय।
क्षण क्षण का उपयोग कर,
बीता क्षण नहीं आय।।

Kṣaṇa kṣaṇa kṣaṇa kṣaṇa bītate,
jīvana bītā jāya.
Kṣaṇa kṣaṇa kā upayoga kara,
bītā kṣaṇa nahīṅ āya.

SIDE B

६२

मानव का जीवन मिला,
धर्म मिला अनमोल।
अब श्रद्धा से यतन से,
अपने बंधन खोल।।

Mānava kā jīvana milā,
Dharma milā anamola.
Aba śraddhā se yatana se,
apane bandhana khola.

६३

मानव जीवन रतन सा,
किया व्यर्थ बरबाद।
चरचा कर ली धरम की,
चाख न पाया स्वाद।।

Mānava jīvana ratana sā,
kiyā vyartha barabāda.
Caracā kara lī Dharama kī,
cākha na pāyā svāda.

60
May Dhamma arise every moment,
may awareness arise every moment.
May no moment be of ignorance,
may no intoxication or heedlessness remain.

61
Moment after moment after moment,
life keeps slipping by.
Make use of every moment;
the moment past never comes again.

SIDE B

62
Attained—this human life;
attained—the priceless Dhamma.
Now with faith and effort
to untie your bonds!

63
Human life is like a jewel
that you have idly squandered.
Merely talking of Dhamma,
you did not taste its savor.

६४

जीवन सारा खो दिया,
ग्रंथ पढ़ंत-पढ़ंत।
तोते मैना की तरह,
नाम रटंत-रटंत।।

Jīvana sārā kho diyā,
grantha paḍhanta-paḍhanta.
Tote mainā kī taraha,
nāma raṭanta-raṭanta.

६५

कितने दिन यों ही गए,
करते वाद विवाद!
अवसर आया धरम का,
चाख धरम का स्वाद।।

Kitane dina yoṅ hī gae,
karate vāda vivāda.
Avasara āyā Dharama kā,
cākha Dharama kā svāda.

६६

दुरलभ जीवन मनुज का,
दुरलभ धरम मिलाप।
धन्य भाग! दोनों मिले,
दूर करें भव ताप।।

Duralabha jīvana manuja kā,
duralabha Dharama milāpa.
Dhanya bhāga! donoṅ mile,
dūra kareṅ bhava tāpa.

६७(क)

जीवन सारा खो दिया,
करते बुद्धि-विलास।
बुद्धि-विलासों से भला,
किसकी बुझती प्यास।।

Jīvana sārā kho diyā,
karate buddhi-vilāsa.
Buddhi-vilāsoṅ se bhalā
kisakī bujhatī pyāsa?

64
All your life is wasted
in reading book after book,
like a parrot or mynah
that repeats names by rote.

65
So many days have passed
in discussions and debates!
The time has come for Dhamma;
taste the savor of Dhamma.

66
Rare is human life,
rare to encounter the Dhamma.
We are fortunate to have both;
let us banish the torment of becoming.

67a
All of life is wasted
in playing intellectual games.
By intellectual games
whose thirst has been quenched?

६७(ख)

मत कर मत कर बावले!	Mata kara mata kara bāvale!
मत कर बुद्धि-विलास।	Mata kara buddhi-vilāsa.
बुद्धि-विलासों से भला,	Buddhi-vilāsoṅ se bhalā,
किसकी बुझती प्यास।।	kisakī bujhatī pyāsa?

६८

चरचा ही चरचा करे,	Caracā hī caracā kare,
धारण करे न कोय।	dhāraṇa kare na koya.
धर्म बिचारा क्या करे,	Dharma bicārā kyā kare?
धारे ही सुख होय।।	Dhāre hī sukha hoya.

६९

धारण करे तो धर्म है,	Dhāraṇa kare to Dharma hai,
वरना कोरी बात।	varanā korī bāta.
सूरज उगे प्रभात है,	Sūraja uge prabhāta hai,
वरना काली रात।।	varanā kālī rāta.

७०

आते जाते सांस पर,	Āte jāte sāṅsa para,
रहे निरंतर ध्यान।	rahe nirantara dhyāna.
कर्मों के बंधन कटें,	Karmoṅ ke bandhana kaṭeṅ,
होय परम कल्याण।।	hoya parama kalyāṇa.

67b

Don't do it, child, don't do it!
Don't play intellectual games.
By intellectual games
whose thirst has been quenched?

68

They only talk and talk of it,
but nobody applies it.
Poor Dhamma! What can it do?
Its practice alone brings happiness.

69

If you apply it, it is Dhamma;
otherwise it is empty talk.
When the sun rises, dawn comes;
otherwise, blackest night.

70

In-breath, out-breath—
if you keep unbroken awareness,
the knots of *kamma* will be sundered,
leading to the highest welfare.

७१

सांस देखते देखते,	Sāṅsa dekhate dekhate,
मन अविचल हो जाय।	mana avicala ho jāya.
अविचल मन निरमल बने,	Avicala mana niramala bane,
सहज मुक्त हो जाय।।	sahaja mukta ho jāya.

७२

सांस देखते देखते,	Sāṅsa dekhate dekhate,
सत्य प्रकटता जाय।	satya prakaṭatā jāya.
सत्य देखते देखते,	Satya dekhate dekhate,
परम सत्य दिख जाय।।	parama satya dikha jāya.

७३

पल पल क्षण क्षण होश रख,	Pala pala kṣaṇa kṣaṇa hośa rakha,
अपना कर्म सुधार।	apanā karma sudhāra.
सुख से जीने की कला,	Sukha se jīne kī kalā,
अपनी ओर निहार।।	apanī ora nihāra.

७४

क्षण क्षण प्रतिक्षण सजग रह,	Kṣaṇa kṣaṇa pratikṣaṇa sajaga raha,
अपना होश संभाल।	apanā hośa sambhāla.
राग द्वेष की प्रतिक्रिया,	Rāga dveṣa kī pratikriyā,
टाल सके तो टाल।।	ṭāla sake to ṭāla.

71
Observing breath after breath,
the mind becomes still.
Unwavering, the mind becomes pure
and naturally finds liberation.

72
As you observe breath after breath
the truth reveals itself.
Observing truth after truth
you come to ultimate truth.

73
Moment by moment keep your sanity,
rectify your own actions.
This is the art of living happily
by observing yourself.

74
Moment by moment remain alert,
guard your sanity.
Strive to avoid and fend off
the reactions of craving and aversion.

७५

बीते क्षण तो चल दिए,
आने वाले दूर।
इस क्षण में जो भी जीए,
वो ही साधक शूर।।

Bīte kṣaṇa to cala die,
āne-vāle dūra.
Isa kṣaṇa meṅ jo bhī jīe,
vo hī sādhaka śūra.

७६

समय बड़ा अनमोल है,
समय न हाट बिकाय।
तीन लोक संपद दिये,
बीता क्षण न पाय।।

Samaya baḍā anamola hai,
samaya na hāṭa bikāya.
Tīna loka sampada diye,
bītā kṣaṇa na pāya.

७७

बीते क्षण को याद कर,
मत बिरथा अकुळाय।
बीता धन तो मिल सके,
बीता क्षण नहीं आय।।

Bīte kṣaṇa ko yāda kara,
mata birathā akuḷāya.
Bītā dhana to mila sake,
bītā kṣaṇa nahīṅ āya.

७८

भूतकाल व्याकुल करे,
या भविष्य भरमाय।
वर्तमान में जो जिए,
तो जीना आ जाय।।

Bhūtakāla vyākula kare,
yā bhaviṣya bharamāya.
Vartamāna meṅ jo jie,
to jīnā ā jāya.

75
Past moments are gone,
those to come are far away.
Whoever lives in this moment
is a meditator of courage.

76
Time is so precious,
time is not for sale in the market.
Even for the wealth of three worlds
you can't buy back the moment past.

77
Remembering past moments,
don't uselessly be obsessed.
Past wealth can be recovered but
past moments can never return.

78
Living in the past is agitating,
living in the future is delusory.
If you live in the present,
you have learnt how to live.

७९
प्रतिक्षण अंतर तप चले,
प्रतिक्षण रह निषपाप।
प्रतिक्षण बंधनमुक्त हों,
दूर करें भव ताप।।

Pratikṣaṇa antara tapa cale,
pratikṣaṇa raha niṣapāpa.
Pratikṣaṇa bandhanamukta hoṅ,
dūra kareṅ bhava tāpa.

८०
तप रे तप रे मानवी,
तपे ही निर्मल होय।
सुबरण भट्ठी में तपे,
तप तप कुंदन होय।।

Tapa re, tapa re mānavī,
tape hī nirmala hoya.
Subaraṇa bhaṭṭhī meṅ tape,
tapa tapa kundana hoya.

८१
नए करम बांधे नहीं,
क्षीण पुरातन होय।
क्षण क्षण जाग्रत ही रहे,
सहज मुक्त है सोय।।

Nae karama bāndhe nahīṅ,
kṣīṇa purātana hoya.
Kṣaṇa kṣaṇa jāgrata hī rahe,
sahaja mukta hai soya.

८२
देख देख कर चित्त की,
ग्रंथि सुलझती जाय।
जागे विमल विपश्यना,
चित्त मुक्त हो जाय।।

Dekha dekha kara citta kī,
granthi sulajhatī jāya.
Jāge vimala Vipaśyanā,
citta mukta ho jāya.

79
Every moment purify within,
every moment keep away from evil,
every moment free yourself of bonds
to vanquish the torments of existence.

80
Strive ardently, oh man, and burn!
Purity comes from burning away the dross.
Gold must pass through a crucible
in order to be refined.

81
Do not generate new *kamma*,
let the old be extinguished,
every moment remain vigilant,
and naturally you become liberated.

82
Observe the mind steadfastly
to disentangle its knots.
May stainless Vipassana arise
to liberate the mind.

८३

बाहर बाहर भटकते,
दुखिया रहे जहान।
अंतरमन में खोज ली,
सुख की खान खदान।।

Bāhara bāhara bhaṭakate,
dukhiyā rahe jahāna.
Antaramana meṅ khoja lī,
sukha kī khāna khadāna.

८४

होश जगे जब धरम का,
होवे दूर प्रमाद।
स्वदर्शन करते हुए,
चखे मुक्ति का स्वाद।।

Hośa jage jaba Dharama kā,
hove dūra pramāda.
Svadarśana karate hue,
cakhe mukti kā svāda.

८५

तृष्णा जड़ से खोद कर,
अनासक्त बन जांय।
भव बंधन से छुटन का,
यही एक उपाय।।

Tṛṣṇā jaḍa se khoda kara,
anāsakta bana jāṅya.
Bhava bandhana se chuṭana kā,
yahī eka upāya.

८६

भोगत भोगत भोगते,
बंधन बंधते जांय।
देखत देखत देखते,
बंधन खुलते जांय।।

Bhogata bhogata bhogate,
bandhana bandhate jāṅya.
Dekhata dekhata dekhate,
bandhana khulate jāṅya.

83
Always straying outward,
the world remains miserable.
By searching the depths of the mind
you tap the treasure-lode of happiness.

84
When the clarity of Dhamma arises,
delusion is dispelled.
Observing yourself,
you taste the savor of liberation.

85
Dig out craving by the roots
and become detached.
This is the only way
to break the bonds of becoming.

86
Rolling, rolling in pleasure and pain,
we keep tying knots.
Observing, observing, observing,
we open all the knots.

८७

ऐसी जगे विपश्यना,
समता चित्त समाय।
एक एक कर पाप की,
परत उतरती जाय।।

Aisī jage Vipaśyanā,
samatā citta samāya.
Eka eka kara pāpa kī
parata utaratī jāya.

८८

ज्यों ज्यों अंतरजगत में,
समता छाती जाय।
काया वाणी चित्त के,
करम सुधरते जांय।।

Jyoṅ jyoṅ antarajagata meṅ,
samatā chātī jāya.
Kāyā vāṇī citta ke,
karama sudharate jāṅya.

८९

बाहर भीतर एकरस,
सरल स्वच्छ व्यवहार।
कथनी करनी एक सी,
यही धरम का सार।।

Bāhara bhītara ekarasa,
sarala svaccha vyavahāra.
Kathanī karanī eka sī,
yahī Dharama kā sāra.

९०

कपट रहे ना कुटिलता,
रहे न मिथ्याचार।
शुद्ध धरम ऐसा जगे,
जगे स्वच्छ व्यवहार।।

Kapaṭa rahe nā kuṭilatā,
rahe na mithyācāra.
Śuddha Dharama aisā jage,
jage svaccha vyavahāra.

87
May Vipassana thus arise
to suffuse the mind with equanimity.
One after another, may each layer
of negativity be stripped away.

88
As in the inner world
equanimity spreads,
the actions of body, speech
and mind are transformed.

89
Inside and outside alike,
straight and clean in dealings;
oneness in words and deeds—
this is the essence of Dhamma.

90
Let there be no deceit or malice,
let there be no wrong action.
Let pure Dhamma arise,
making your conduct upright.

९१

शीलवान के ध्यान से,
प्रज्ञा जाग्रत होय।
चित समता में स्थित होवे,
उत्तम मंगल होय।।

Śīlavāna ke dhyāna se,
pragyā jāgrata hoya.
Cita samatā meṅ sthita hove,
uttama maṅgala hoya.

९२

जिसके मन प्रज्ञा जगे,
होय विनम्र विनीत।
जिस डाली पर फल लगें,
झुकने की ही रीत।।

Jisake mana pragyā jage,
hoya vinamra vinīta.
Jisa ḍālī para phala lageṅ,
jhukane kī hī rīta.

९३

धन आए तो बावरे,
मत कर गरब गुमान।
यह बालू की भींत है,
इसका क्या अभिमान।।

Dhana āe to bāvare,
mata kara garaba gumāna.
Yaha bālū kī bhīnta hai,
isakā kyā abhimāna?

९४

मत कर मत कर बावरे!
अहंकार अभिमान।
बड़ों बड़ों का मिट गया,
जग से नाम निशान।।

Mata kara mata kara bāvare!
Ahaṅkāra abhimāna.
Baḍoṅ baḍoṅ kā miṭa gayā,
jaga se nāma niśāna.

91
When a person of morality concentrates,
insight awakens.
The mind becomes steadfast in equanimity;
this is the greatest happiness.

92
If wisdom arises in your mind
you become humble and modest,
as a branch laden with fruit
is sure to bow low.

93
If wealth comes, oh child,
do not be vain and haughty.
It is a castle made of sand;
why be proud of it?

94
Don't do it, child, don't do it!
Don't be proud and haughty.
All trace of the high and mighty
has vanished from the world.

९५

सुख आए नाचे नहीं,
दुख आए नहीं रोय।
दोनों में समरस रहे,
धरमवंत है सोय।।

Sukha āe nāce nahīṅ,
dukha āe nahīṅ roya.
Donoṅ meṅ samarasa rahe,
Dharamavanta hai soya.

९६

सुख दुख आते ही रहें,
ज्यों आवें दिन रैन।
तू क्यूं खोवे बावळा,
अपने मन की चैन।।

Sukha dukha āte hī raheṅ,
jyoṅ āveṅ dina raina.
Tū kyūṅ khove bāvaḷā,
apane mana kī caina?

९७

अनचाही होवे कभी,
मनचाही भी होय।
धूप छांह की जिंदगी,
क्या नाचे क्या रोय।।

Anacāhī hove kabhī,
manacāhī bhī hoya.
Dhūpa chāṅha kī jindagī,
kyā nāce kyā roya?

९८

जीवन में आते रहें,
पतझड़ और बसंत।
चित विचलित होवे नहीं,
मंगल जगे अनंत।।

Jīvana meṅ āte raheṅ,
patajhaḍa aura basanta.
Cita vicalita hove nahīṅ,
maṅgala jage ananta.

95
Not dancing when pleasure comes,
not wailing when in pain,
keeping equilibrium with both—
this is living the Dhamma.

96
Pleasure and pain keep coming
like day and night.
Why then cast away
your peace of mind, oh child?

97
Unwanted things may come our way,
wanted things as well.
Life contains both light and shade.
Then why dance? Why weep?

98
In life there keep coming
autumns and springs.
If the mind does not waver,
you enjoy infinite happiness.

९९

कभी बाग वीरान है,
कभी बसंत बहार।
समता में प्रमुदित रहे,
संत निहार निहार।।

Kabhī bāga vīrāna hai,
kabhī basanta bahāra.
Samatā meṅ pramudita rahe,
santa nihāra nihāra.

१००

तन सुख, धन सुख, मान सुख,
भले ध्यान सुख होय।
पर समता सुख परम सुख,
अतुल अपरिमित होय।।

Tana sukha, dhana sukha, māna sukha
bhale dhyāna sukha hoya.
Para samatā sukha parama sukha,
atula aparimita hoya.

१०१

अंतर में डुबकी लगी,
भीग गए सब अंग।
धरम रंग ऐसा चढ़ा,
चढ़े न दूजा रंग।।

Antara meṅ ḍubakī lagī,
bhīga gae saba aṅga.
Dharama raṅga aisā caḍhā,
caḍhe na dūjā raṅga.

१०२

जैसे मेरे दुख कटे,
सबके दुख कट जांय।
जैसे मेरे दिन फिरे,
सबके दिन फिर जांय।।

Jaise mere dukha kaṭe,
sabake dukha kaṭa jāṅya.
Jaise mere dina phire,
sabake dina phira jāṅya.

99
At times the garden withers,
at times spring makes it bloom.
Remaining joyful with equanimity,
the saint simply observes.

100
Better than pleasures of the senses, wealth or reputation
is the happiness of concentration,
but best is the happiness of equanimity,
beyond compare or limit.

101
By plunging deep within,
the entire being has become so saturated
with the color of the Dhamma
that no other color can impinge.

102
As my suffering was cut off,
may the suffering of all be ended.
As my life was renewed,
may that of all be changed.

१०३

मेरे सुख में शांति में,	Mere sukha meṅ śānti meṅ,
भाग सभी का होय।	bhāga sabhī kā hoya.
इस मंगलमय धरम का,	Isa maṅgalamaya Dharama kā,
लाभ सभी को होय।।	lābha sabhī ko hoya.

१०४

इस दुखियारे जगत में,	Isa dukhiyāre jagata meṅ
सुखिया दिखे न कोय।	sukhiyā dikhe na koya.
शुद्ध धरम जग में जगे,	Śuddha Dharama jaga meṅ jage,
जन जन सुखिया होय।।	jana jana sukhiyā hoya.

१०५

शुद्ध धरम इस जगत में,	Śuddha Dharama isa jagata meṅ,
पुनः प्रतिष्ठित होय।	punaḥ pratiṣṭhita hoya.
जन जन का होवे भला,	Jana jana kā hove bhalā,
जन जन मंगल होय।।	jana jana maṅgala hoya.

१०६

जग में बहती ही रहे,	Jaga meṅ bahatī hī rahe,
धरम गंग की धार।	Dharama Gaṅga kī dhāra.
जन जन का होवे भला,	Jana jana kā hove bhalā,
जन जन का उपकार।।	jana jana kā upakāra.

103
May my happiness and peace
be shared by one and all.
May this munificent Dhamma
benefit one and all.

104
In this wretched world
I see no one who is happy.
May pure Dhamma arise in the world,
bringing happiness to all.

105
Again may the pure Dhamma
be established in the world,
bringing welfare to many,
bringing happiness to many.

106
May the Ganges of the Dhamma
keep flowing in the world,
for the happiness of everyone,
for the benefit of all.

१०७

भला होय इस जगत का,
सुखी होंय सब लोग।
दूर होंय दारिद्र दुख,
दूर होंय सब रोग।।

Bhalā hoya isa jagata kā,
sukhī hoṅya saba loga.
Dūra hoṅya dāridra dukha,
dūra hoṅya saba roga.

१०८

बरसे बरखा समय पर,
दूर रहे दुषकाल।
शासन होवे धरम का,
लोग होंय खुशहाल।।

Barase barakhā samaya para,
dūra rahe duṣakāla.
Śāsana hove Dharama kā,
loga hoṅya khuśahāla.

१०९

शासन में जागे धरम,
उखड़े भ्रष्टाचार।
धनियों में जागे धरम,
स्वच्छ होय व्यापार।।

Śāsana meṅ jāge Dharama,
ukhaḍe bhraṣṭācāra.
Dhaniyoṅ meṅ jāge Dharama,
svaccha hoya vyāpāra.

११०

जन जन में जागे धरम,
जन जन सुखिया होय।
जन मन के दुखड़े मिटें,
जन जन मंगल होय।।

Jana jana meṅ jāge Dharama,
jana jana sukhiyā hoya.
Jana mana ke dukhaḍe miṭeṅ,
jana jana maṅgala hoya.

107
May the world enjoy well-being;
may all people be happy.
May poverty and suffering be dispelled;
may all ills be vanquished.

108
May the rains fall in due season,
may there be no drought.
May the government be righteous,
may the people be happy and prosperous.

109
May Dhamma arise among the rulers,
uprooting corruption.
May Dhamma arise in the wealthy,
cleansing business dealings.

110
May the Dhamma arise in the masses,
may everyone be happy.
May affliction be ended in the minds of all;
may all be at peace.

१११

दुखियारे दुखमुक्त हों,
भय त्यागें भयभीत।
बैर छोड़ कर लोग सब,
करें परस्पर प्रीत।।

Dukhiyāre dukhamukta hoṅ,
bhaya tyāgeṅ bhayabhīta.
Baira choḍa kara loga saba,
kareṅ paraspara prīta.

११२

द्वेष और दुरभाव का,
रहे न नाम निशान।
स्नेह और सदभाव से,
भर लें तन मन प्राण।।

Dveṣa aura durabhāva kā
rahe na nāma niśāna.
Sneha aura sadabhāva se,
bhara leṅ tana mana prāṇa.

११३

दूर रहे दुरभावना,
द्वेष होंय सब दूर।
निरमल निरमल चित्त में,
प्यार भरे भरपूर।।

Dūra rahe durabhāvanā,
dveṣa hoṅya saba dūra.
Niramala niramala citta meṅ,
pyāra bhare bharapūra.

११४

ज्यों इकलौते पूत पर,
उमड़े मां का प्यार।
त्यों प्यारा लगता रहे,
हमें सकल संसार।।

Jyoṅ ikalaute pūta para,
umaḍe māṅ kā pyāra.
Tyoṅ pyārā lagatā rahe,
hameṅ sakala saṅsāra.

111
May the wretched be freed of suffering,
may the fearful be rid of fear.
May all people forsake enmity;
may they love each other.

112
Of hatred and ill will
may not a trace remain.
May love and good will
fill body, mind and life.

113
May ill will be far away,
may all aversion be dispelled.
May the pure and stainless heart
brim over with love.

114
As a mother overflows with love
for her only son,
may we keep feeling love
for all the universe.

११५

दुखी देख करुणा जगे,	Dukhī dekha karuṇā jage,
सुखी देख मन मोद।	sukhī dekha mana moda.
मंगल मैत्री से भरे,	Maṅgala maitrī se bhare,
अंतस ओतपरोत।।	antasa otaparota.

११६

दृष्य और अदृष्य सब,	Dṛṣya aura adṛṣya saba,
प्राणी सुखिया हों‍य।	prāṇī sukhiyā hoṅya.
निरमल हो निरबैर हों,	Niramala ho, nirabaira hoṅ,
सभी निरामय हों‍य।।	sabhī nirāmaya hoṅya.

११७(क)

दसों दिशाओं के सभी,	Dasoṅ diśāoṅ ke sabhī,
प्राणी सुखिया हों‍य।	prāṇī sukhiyā hoṅya.
निरभय हों, निरबैर हों,	Nirabhaya hoṅ, nirabaira hoṅ,
सभी निरामय हों‍य।।	sabhī nirāmaya hoṅya.

११७(ख)

जल के, थल के, गगन के,	Jala ke, thala ke, gagana ke,
प्राणी सुखिया हों‍य।	prāṇī sukhiyā hoṅya.
निरभय हों, निरबैर हों,	Nirabhaya hoṅ, nirabaira hoṅ,
सभी निरामय हों‍य।।	sabhī nirāmaya hoṅya.

115
Seeing the wretched, may compassion arise;
seeing the happy, joy.
May the depths of the mind be filled and permeated
with infinite love and good will.

116
Visible or invisible,
may all beings be happy,
pure-minded, without enmity;
may all be freed of ills.

117a
In the ten directions,
may beings be happy,
without fear or enmity;
may all be freed of ills.

117b
Whether of water, earth or sky,
may beings be happy,
without fear or enmity;
may all be freed of ills.

११८(क)

सुख छाए संसार में,	Sukha chāe saṅsāra meṅ,
दुखिया रहे न कोय।	dukhiyā rahe na koya.
जन जन मन जागे धरम,	Jana jana mana jāge Dharama,
जन जन सुखिया होय।।	jana jana sukhiyā hoya.

११८(ख)

सुख व्यापे इस जगत में,	Sukha vyāpe isa jagata meṅ,
दुखिया रहे न कोय।	dukhiyā rahe na koya.
जन जन मन जागे धरम,	Jana jana mana jāge Dharama,
जन जन सुखिया होय।	jana jana sukhiyā hoya.
जन जन मंगल होय,	Jana jana maṅgala hoya,
सबका मंगल होय।।	sabakā maṅgala hoya.

भवतु सब्ब मंगलं	*Bhavatu sabba maṅgalaṃ.*
साधु साधु साधु	*Sādhu, sādhu, sādhu.*

118a
May happiness spread through the universe,
may no one remain wretched,
may the Dhamma arise in the minds of all,
may everyone be contented.

118b
May happiness spread through the world,
may no one remain wretched,
may the Dhamma arise in the minds of all,
may everyone be contented,
may everyone be happy,
may all be happy.

May all beings be happy.
Well said, well said, well said.

NOTES

Verses 28-29

The reference here is to the three sacred rivers of India: the Ganges, the Jamuna and the mythical Saraswati. According to traditional Hindu belief, pilgrims can wash away their sins by bathing in the water at the point where the rivers join.

Verse 117a

The ten directions are east, southeast, south, southwest, west, northwest, north, northeast, above and below.